A Toulouse Story

Anne Irwin Nichols

AuthorHouse™
1663 Liberty Drive
Bloomington, IN 47403
www.authorhouse.com
Phone: 1 (800) 839-8640

© 2016 Anne Irwin Nichols. All rights reserved.

No part of this book may be reproduced, stored in a retrieval system, or transmitted by any means without the written permission of the author.

This is a work of fiction. All of the characters, names, incidents, organizations, and dialogue in this novel are either the products of the author's imagination or are used fictitiously.

Published by AuthorHouse 01/26/2016

ISBN: 978-1-5049-7537-7 (sc)
ISBN: 978-1-5049-7531-5 (e)

Print information available on the last page.

Any people depicted in stock imagery provided by Thinkstock are models, and such images are being used for illustrative purposes only.
Certain stock imagery © Thinkstock.

This book is printed on acid-free paper.

Because of the dynamic nature of the Internet, any web addresses or links contained in this book may have changed since publication and may no longer be valid. The views expressed in this work are solely those of the author and do not necessarily reflect the views of the publisher, and the publisher hereby disclaims any responsibility for them.

authorHOUSE®

Mama Goose sat on her clutch.

She kept them warm for two months.

Then one warm spring day the eggshells began to...

CRACK...
CRACK...
CRACK...
CRACK...

First---you see a tiny yellow <u>bill</u> poking through the top of an egg.

Second---you see a yellow-grayed head pop out of the shell.

Third---you see a wriggling body pushed out of the eggshell.

Fourth---you see a pair of webbed orange feet flaying around the bottom of the eggshell.

Now, more of the eggs are cracked.

Goslings are pushing out of their eggshell homes.

They have <u>hatched</u>!

The warm spring sunshine dries their <u>down</u>.

They also flap their wing to help dry the <u>down</u>.

The goslings <u>feathers</u> do not begin to grow for a few weeks.

The goslings are *not* waterproof until the <u>feathers</u> begin to grow.

Mama Goose keeps the goslings under her <u>feathers</u> and <u>down</u> to keep them warm.

Papa Goose waddles over to see the newly hatched goslings.

Geese are VERY <u>territorial</u> at nesting time.

The <u>Gander</u> **honks** and hisses and *chases* away anything that comes close to his babies!

The Goose and the Gander will chase away the farmers who feed them!

The Gander is a VERY good <u>protector</u>.

The third day after hatching the gosling are getting **hungry** and **thirsty**.

The yolk in the egg feeds them for TWO days.

Mama Goose starts to walk to the pond.

ALL the goslings follow her.

They DO NOT line up in a line like ducklings.

These babies follow NO ONE!

Each likes to go their OWN WAY!

BUT, you need to watch out should any animal come close to them...

Mama and Papa Goose will **honk**, *hiss*, **chase**, and bite if you get too close!

When leaving their <u>nest</u> they climb over rocks and stones.

They also <u>trudge</u> through tall grass and weeds.

The smell of water causes them to run!

OOPS! Some of them fell trying to hurry.

Scrambling to get up and stay with Mama and Papa is NOT easy.

Rest time is needed for these young goslings.

They dropped down to the ground for a breather.

Then they chewed on some fresh, green grass.

As they become older they will eat a lot of grass and weeds.

Toulouse Geese are a very placid type of geese.

They make a great farm and ranch goose.

The goslings follow Mama Goose to the pond.

They watch Mama put her bill into the water, then put her head up and swallow the water.

Then Papa has a drink of pond water.

Each gosling took drinks of water like their parents did.

Mama oiled the goslings <u>down</u> so they could get in the water.

If their <u>down</u> is not oiled, they will sink and not be able to swim.

When the feathers grow in, so will the oil.

Later the yellow-gray <u>down</u> will be covered in white and gray feathers.

Then they can swim in the pond or lake.

They have so much FUN taking a bath!

NOW, it was time to walk to the barnyard to eat some grain.

The farmer had scattered grain on the ground for the geese to eat.

The Goslings liked the taste of the different grains.

The grain has grit in it that will help the geese digest their food.

It's time the young family to return to the nest for a rest.

A Toulouse Story

In the fall and winter the geese can stand cold temperatures because their feathers cover the down.

In the spring they will build nests from grass and leaves.

The babies have grown UP.

Now they have their own clutch.

When there is more than five geese together on the ground they are called a gaggle.

If they fly, geese are called a skein.

The Toulouse Geese are usually too heavy to fly.

They can get three to four feet off the ground for a short time.

A Toulouse Story

Toulouse geese are named for the town Toulouse, France.

Over four hundred years ago in 1555 it was first written gray and white gentle geese were used on farms.

You can eat their eggs the same as chicken eggs!

ALL geese are <u>monogamous</u>.

Toulouse geese make WONDERFUL pets!

A Toulouse Story

GLOSSARY

bill- the horny part of the jaws of a bird, a beak (mouth area)

clutch-a nest of eggs

down-a covering of soft, fluffy, feathers

feathers-the light horny outer covering the body of birds

gaggle-a flock of more than five geese, when not in flight

gander-an adult male goose

goose-any one of many different kinds of birds that swim, that are larger than ducks, and that have long necks; a female goose

grain-the seeds of plants that are used for food

grit-very small pieces of sand or stone

monogamous-the state of being married to only one person @ a time during a life time

nest-the place where a bird lays its eggs and takes care of its young

placid-not easily upset or excited; calm or steady

pond-an area of water surrounded by land that is smaller than a lake

protector-a person or thing that protects someone or something

skein-a flock of wildfowl (as geese or ducks) in flight

territorial-animals or people that try to keep others away from an area that they use or control

yolk-a mass of stored food, surrounded by the white in an egg; the yellow in center of as yolk